The Poetry of Horses

The Poetry of Horses

By the World's Greatest Poets

First published in Great Britain in 2021 by
Serpent's Tail
an imprint of Profile Books Ltd
29 Cloth Fair
London
EC1A 7JQ

www.serpentstail.com

Collection edited by Leonora Craig Cohen

Text design by Sue Lamble

1 3 5 7 9 10 8 6 4 2

Typeset in Quadraat by MacGuru Ltd
Printed and bound in Great Britain by
CPI Group (UK) Ltd, Croydon, CR0 4YY

The moral right of the author has been asserted.

A CIP catalogue record for this book is
available from the British Library.

ISBN 978 1 78816 604 1
eISBN 978 1 78283 745 9

Contents

WILLIAM HENRY OGILVIE

The Horse of Your Heart

When you've ridden a four-year-old half of the day
And, foam to the fetlock, they lead him away,
With a sigh of contentment you watch him depart
While you tighten the girths on the horse of your
  heart.
There is something between you that both
  understand
As it thrills an old message from bit-bar to hand.
As he changes his feet in that plunge of desire
To the thud of his hoofs all your courage takes fire.
When an afternoon fox is away, when begins
The rush down the headland that edges the whins,
When you challenge the Field, making sure of a
  start,
Would you ask any horse but this horse of your
  heart?
There's the rasping big double a green one would
  shirk,
But the old fellow knows it as part of his work;
He has shortened his stride, he has measured the
  task,
He is up, on, and over as clean as you'd ask.
There's the water before you-no novice's test,

But a jump to try deeply the boldest and best;
Just a tug at the leather, a lift of the ear,
And the old horse is over it-twenty foot clear.
There is four foot of wall and a take-off in plough,
And you're glad you are riding no tenderfoot now
But a seasoned campaigner, a master of art,
The perfect performer-the horse of your heart.
For here's where the raw one will falter and baulk,
And here's where the tyro is pulled to a walk,
But the horse of your heart never dwells or demurs
And is over the top to a touch of the spurs.
To you who ride young ones half-schooled and half-
   broke,
What joy to find freedom a while from your yoke!
What bliss to be launched with the luck of the start
On the old one, the proved one, the horse of your
   heart !

JENNIFER CHANG

A Horse Named Never

At the stables, each stall was labeled with a name.
Biscuit stood aloof—I faced, always, invariably, his
    clockwork tail.
Crab knew the salt lick too well.
Trapezoid mastered stillness: a midnight mare,
    she was sternest and tallest, her chest stretched
    against the edges of her stall.
I was not afraid of Never, the chestnut gelding, so
    rode his iron haunches as far as Panther Gap.
Never and I lived in Virginia then.
We could neither flee nor be kept.
Seldom did I reach the little mountain without
    him, the easy crests making valleys of indifferent
    grasses.
What was that low sound I heard, alone with Never?
A lone horse, a lodestar, a habit of fear.
We think of a horse less as the history of one man and his
    sorrows than as the history of a whole evil time.
Why I chose Never I'll never know.
I fed him odd lettuce, abundant bitterness.
Who wore the bit and harness, who was the ready
    steed.
Never took the carrot, words by my own reckoning,

an account of creeks and oystercatchers.

Our hoof-house rested at the foot of the mountain,
   on which rested another house more brazen than
   statuary.

Let it be known: I first mistook gelding for gilding.

I am the fool that has faith in Never.

Somewhere, a gold door burdened with apology
   refuses all mint from the yard.

PHILIP LARKIN

At Grass

The eye can hardly pick them out
From the cold shade they shelter in,
Till wind distresses tail and mane;
Then one crops grass, and moves about
– The other seeming to look on –
And stands anonymous again.

Yet fifteen years ago, perhaps
Two dozen distances sufficed
To fable them: faint afternoons
Of Cups and Stakes and Handicaps,
Whereby their names were artificed
To inlay faded, classic Junes –

Silks at the start: against the sky
Numbers and parasols: outside,
Squadrons of empty cars, and heat,
And littered grass: then the long cry
Hanging unhushed till it subside
To stop-press columns on the street.

Do memories plague their ears like flies?
They shake their heads. Dusk brims the shadows.

Summer by summer all stole away,
The starting-gates, the crowds and cries –
All but the unmolesting meadows.
Almanacked, their names live; they

Have slipped their names, and stand at ease,
Or gallop for what must be joy,
And not a fieldglass sees them home,
Or curious stopwatch prophesies:
Only the groom, and the groom's boy,
With bridles in the evening come.

MATTHEA HARVEY

Inside the Good Idea

From the outside it is singular. One wooden horse.
Inside ten men sit cross-legged, knees touching. No
noun has been invented yet to describe this. They
whisper that it would be like sitting in a wine barrel
if the curved walls were painted red. The contents
are not content. They would like some wine. They
quarrel about who gets to sit in the head until finally
the smallest man clambers in, promising to send
messages back to the belly. He can only look out of
one eye at a time. At first there is nothing to report.
Black, Dark, The Occasional Star. Then Quiet
Footsteps mixed with Questions. The children are
clamoring for it to be brought inside the walls. The
head sends back another message which gets caught
in the throat: *They are bringing their toy horses to pay
their respects to us, brushing their tiny manes, oiling the
little wheels. It must be a welcome change from playing war.*

CAROL ANN DUFFY

The White Horses

The earth's heart hears hooves
under hillsides,

           thunder in Wiltshire;
and the glistening rain, in wet hours,
all ears for the white horses, listens;
the wind, hoarse, gargles
breath and whinny and shriek.
The moon's chalk face pines for her foals.

But the sky swears

           the white horses
are dropped clouds;
the sea vows they came from a wave,
foamy, salt-maned, galloping inland;
death claims it will set them
to pulling a hearse

           and love
goes riding, all night, bareback
hunting itself.

They dreamed them, the local dead,
ghosts of war horses,

           warriors', heroes',

asleep in the landscape;
woke to the white horses shining
high over woods and farms;
young ancestors working the fields,
naming them his, hers, ours.
They sensed them, pulling the county
deep into England,
harnessed, history's;
              their scent sweet on the air –
wheat, hops, hay, chalk, clay.
Then stars nailed shoes to their hooves.

The conservationists climb the hills
away from their cars,
              new leucippotomists
with implements to scour and groom,
scrub and comb.
              On a clear day,
from twenty miles,
              a driver sees a white horse
printing its fresh, old form on the turf
like a poem.

LAWRENCE FERLINGHETTI

Don't Let That Horse ...

Don't let that horse
                    eat that violin

   cried Chagall's mother

                            But he
                    kept right on
                            painting

And became famous

And kept on painting
                    The Horse With Violin In Mouth

And when he finally finished it
he jumped up upon the horse
                            and rode away
            waving the violin

And then with a low bow gave it
to the first naked nude he ran across

And there were no strings
                            attached

JAMES DICKEY

The Dusk of Horses

Right under their noses, the green
Of the field is paling away
Because of something fallen from the sky.

They see this, and put down
Their long heads deeper in grass
That only just escapes reflecting them

As the dream of a millpond would.
The color green flees over the grass
Like an insect, following the red sun over

The next hill. The grass is white.
There is no cloud so dark and white at once;
There is no pool at dawn that deepens

Their faces and thirsts as this does.
Now they are feeding on solid
Cloud, and, one by one,

With nails as silent as stars among the wood
Hewed down years ago and now rotten,
The stalls are put up around them.

Now if they lean, they come
On wood on any side. Not touching it, they sleep.
No beast ever lived who understood

What happened among the sun's fields,
Or cared why the color of grass
Fled over the hill while he stumbled,

Led by the halter to sleep
On his four taxed, worthy legs.
Each thinks he awakens where

The sun is black on the rooftop,
That the green is dancing in the next pasture,
And that the way to sleep

In a cloud, or in a risen lake,
Is to walk as though he were still
in the drained field standing, head down,

To pretend to sleep when led,
And thus to go under the ancient white
Of the meadow, as green goes

And whiteness comes up through his face
Holding stars and rotten rafters,
Quiet, fragrant, and relieved.

LOUISE GLÜCK

Horse Poem

What does the horse give you
That I cannot give you?

I watch you when you are alone,
When you ride into the field behind the dairy,
Your hands buried in the mare's
Dark mane.

Then I know what lies behind your silence:
Scorn, hatred of me, of marriage. Still,
You want me to touch you; you cry out
As brides cry, but when I look at you I see
There are no children in your body.
Then what is there?

Nothing, I think. Only haste
To die before I die.

In a dream, I watched you ride the horse
Over the dry fields and then
Dismount: you two walked together;
In the dark, you had no shadows.
But I felt them coming toward me

Since at night they go anywhere,
They are their own masters.

Look at me. You think I don't understand?
What is the animal
If not passage out of this life?

RONALD DUNCAN

Ode to a Horse

Where in this wide world can
man find nobility without pride,
friendship without envy or beauty
without vanity? Here, where
grace is laced with muscle, and
strength by gentleness confined.

He serves without servility; he has
fought without enmity. There is
nothing so powerful, nothing less
violent, there is nothing so quick,
nothing more patient.

England's past has been borne on
his back. All our history is his
industry; we are his heirs; he
our inheritance.

How They Brought the Good News from Ghent to Aix

I sprang to the stirrup, and Joris, and he;
I gallop'd, Dirck gallop'd, we gallop'd all three;
'Good speed!' cried the watch, as the gate-bolts
    undrew;
'Speed!' echoed the wall to us galloping through;
Behind shut the postern, the lights sank to rest,
And into the midnight we gallop'd abreast.

Not a word to each other; we kept the great pace
Neck by neck, stride by stride, never changing our
    place;
I turn'd in my saddle and made its girths tight,
Then shorten'd each stirrup, and set the pique right,
Rebuckled the cheek-strap, chain'd slacker the bit,
Nor gallop'd less steadily Roland a whit.

'Twas moonset at starting; but while we drew near
Lokeren, the cocks crew and twilight dawn'd clear;
At Boom, a great yellow star came out to see;
At Düffeld, 'twas morning as plain as could be;
And from Mechelm church-steeple we heard the
    half chime,

So, Joris broke silence with, 'Yet there is time!'

At Aershot, up leap'd of a sudden the sun,
And against him the cattle stood black every one,
To stare thro' the mist at us galloping past,
And I saw my stout galloper Roland at last,
With resolute shoulders, each butting away
The haze, as some bluff river headland its spray:

And his low head and crest, just one sharp ear bent
    back
For my voice, and the other prick'd out on his track;
And one eye's black intelligence,—ever that glance
O'er its white edge at me, his own master, askance!
And the thick heavy spume-flakes which aye and
    anon
His fierce lips shook upwards in galloping on.

By Hasselt, Dirck groan'd; and cried Joris 'Stay
    spur!
Your Roos gallop'd bravely, the fault's not in her,
We 'll remember at Aix'—for one heard the quick
    wheeze
Of her chest, saw the stretch'd neck and staggering
    knees,
And sunk tail, and horrible heave of the flank,
As down on her haunches she shudder'd and sank.

So, we were left galloping, Joris and I,

Past Looz and past Tongres, no cloud in the sky;
The broad sun above laugh'd a pitiless laugh,
'Neath our feet broke the brittle bright stubble like
　　chaff;
Till over by Dalhem a dome-spire sprang white,
And 'Gallop,' gasped Joris, 'for Aix is in sight!'

'How they 'll greet us!'—and all in a moment his
　　roan
Roll'd neck and croup over, lay dead as a stone;
And there was my Roland to bear the whole weight
Of the news which alone could save Aix from her
　　fate,
With his nostrils like pits full of blood to the brim,
And with circles of red for his eye-sockets' rim.

Then I cast loose my buffcoat, each holster let fall,
Shook off both my jack-boots, let go belt and all,
Stood up in the stirrup, lean'd, patted his ear,
Call'd my Roland his pet name, my horse without
　　peer;
Clapp'd my hands, laugh'd and sang, any noise,
　　bad or good,
Till at length into Aix Roland gallop'd and stood.

And all I remember is, friends flocking round
As I sat with his head 'twixt my knees on the
　　ground;
And no voice but was praising this Roland of mine,

As I pour'd down his throat our last measure of
  wine,
Which (the burgesses voted by common consent)
Was no more than his due who brought good news
  from Ghent.

The White Horse

The youth walks up to the white horse, to put its
    halter on
and the horse looks at him in silence.
They are so silent, they are in another world.

Job 39:19–25

Do you give the horse its strength
  or clothe its neck with a flowing mane?
Do you make it leap like a locust,
  striking terror with its proud snorting?
It paws fiercely, rejoicing in its strength,
  and charges into the fray.
It laughs at fear, afraid of nothing;
  it does not shy away from the sword.
The quiver rattles against its side,
  along with the flashing spear and lance.
In frenzied excitement it eats up the ground;
  it cannot stand still when the trumpet sounds.
At the blast of the trumpet it snorts, 'Aha!'
  It catches the scent of battle from afar,
  the shout of commanders and the battle cry.

She Had Some Horses

I. She Had Some Horses

She had some horses.
She had horses who were bodies of sand.
She had horses who were maps drawn of blood.
She had horses who were skins of ocean water.
She had horses who were the blue air of sky.
She had horses who were fur and teeth.
She had horses who were clay and would break.
She had horses who were splintered red cliff.

She had some horses.

She had horses with eyes of trains.
She had horses with full, brown thighs.
She had horses who laughed too much.
She had horses who threw rocks at glass houses.
She had horses who licked razor blades.

She had some horses.

She had horses who danced in their mothers' arms.
She had horses who thought they were the sun and
    their

bodies shone and burned like stars.
She had horses who waltzed nightly on the moon.
She had horses who were much too shy, and kept
  quiet
in stalls of their own making.

She had some horses.

She had horses who liked Creek Stomp Dance
  songs.
She had horses who cried in their beer.
She had horses who spit at male queens who made
them afraid of themselves.
She had horses who said they weren't afraid.
She had horses who lied.
She had horses who told the truth, who were
  stripped
bare of their tongues.

She had some horses.

She had horses who called themselves, 'horse.'
She had horses who called themselves, 'spirit,' and
  kept
their voices secret and to themselves.
She had horses who had no names.
She had horses who had books of names.

She had some horses.

She had horses who whispered in the dark, who
  were afraid to speak.
She had horses who screamed out of fear of the
  silence, who
carried knives to protect themselves from ghosts.
She had horses who waited for destruction.
She had horses who waited for resurrection.

She had some horses.

She had horses who got down on their knees for
  any saviour.
She had horses who thought their high price had
  saved them.
She had horses who tried to save her, who climbed
  in her
bed at night and prayed as they raped her.

She had some horses.

She had some horses she loved.
She had some horses she hated.

These were the same horses.

II. Two Horses

> I thought the sun breaking through
> Sangre de Cristo

Mountains was enough, and that
                    wild musky scents on my body after
          long nights of dreaming could
                              unfold me to myself.
          I thought my dance alone through worlds of
odd and eccentric planets that no one else knew
          would sustain me. I mean
                              I did learn to move
                                        after all
and how to recognize voices other than the most
          familiar.
          But you must have grown out of
                              a thousand years dreaming
          just like I could never imagine you.
                    You must have
                              broke open from another sky
to here, because
                    now I see you as a part of the millions of
          other universes that I thought could never occur
          in this breathing.
                    And I know you as myself, traveling.
In your eyes alone are many colonies of stars
                              and other circling planet motion.
                    And then your fingers, the sweet smell
                    of hair, and
                              your soft, tight belly.
          My heart is taken by you
                    and these mornings since I am a
                    horse running towards

a cracked sky where there are countless dawns
                              breaking simultaneously.
There are two moons on the horizon
and for you
                    I have broken loose.

III. Drowning Horses

She says she is going to kill
herself. I am a thousand miles away.
Listening.
                    To her voice in an ocean
of telephone sound. Grey sky
and nearly sundown; I don't ask her how.
I am already familiar with the weapons:
a restaurant that wouldn't serve her,
the thinnest laughter, another drink.
And even if I weren't closer
to the cliff edge of the talking
wire, I would still be another mirror,
another running horse.

Her escape is my own.
I tell her, yes. Yes. We ride
out for breath over the distance.
Night air approaches, the galloping
other-life.

No sound.
No sound.

IV. Ice Horses

These are the ones who escape
after the last hurt is turned inward;
they are the most dangerous ones.
These are the hottest ones,
but so cold that your tongue sticks
to them and is torn apart because it is
frozen to the motion of hooves.
These are the ones who cut your thighs,
whose blood you must have seen on the gloves
of the doctor's rubber hands. They are
the horses who moaned like oceans, and
one of them a young woman screamed aloud;
she was the only one.
These are the ones who have found you.
These are the ones who pranced on your belly.
They chased deer out of your womb.
These are the ice horses, horses
who entered through your head,
and then your heart,
your beaten heart.

These are the ones who loved you.
They are the horses who have held you
so close that you have become
a part of them,
                 an ice horse
galloping
          into fire.

V. Explosion

The highway near Okemah, Oklahoma exploded

                  They are reasons for everything
Maybe   there is a new people, coming forth
          being born from the center of the earth,
          like us, but another tribe.

Maybe   they will be another color that no one
          has ever seen before. Then they might be
            hated,
          and live in Muskogee on the side of the
            tracks
          that Indians live on. (And they will be the
            ones to save us.)

Maybe   there are lizards coming out of rivers of
            lava
          from the core of this planet,

                  coming to bring rain

      to dance for the corn,
      to set fields of tongues slapping at the dark
      earth, a kind of a dance.

But maybe the explosion was horses,
                bursting out of the crazy earth

near Okemah. They were a violent birth,
flew from the ground into trees
                        to wait for evening night
mares to come after them:

then   into the dank wet fields of Oklahoma
then   their birth cords tied into the molten heart
then   they travel north and south, east and west
then   into wet while sheets at midnight when
          everyone
        sleeps and the baby dreams of swimming in the
        bottom of the muggy river.
then   into frogs who have come out of the earth to
        see for rain
then   a Creek woman who dances shaking the
          seeds in
        her bones
then   South Dakota, Mexico, Japan, and Manila
then   into Miami to sweep away the knived faces
          of hatred

Some will not see them.

But some will see the horses with their hearts of
  sleeping volcanoes
and will be rocked awake
                        past their bodies

                        to see who they have become.

JOHN BUNYAN

Upon the Horse and his Rider

There's one rides very sagely on the road,
Showing that he affects the gravest mode.
Another rides tantivy, or full trot,
To show much gravity he matters not.
Lo, here comes one amain, he rides full speed,
Hedge, ditch, nor miry bog, he doth not heed.
One claws it up-hill without stop or check,
Another down as if he'd break his neck.
Now every horse has his especial guider;
Then by his going you may know the rider.

Comparison.

Now let us turn our horse into a man,
His rider to a spirit, if we can.
Then let us, by the methods of the guider,
Tell every horse how he should know his rider.
Some go, as men, direct in a right way,
Nor are they suffered to go astray;
As with a bridle they are governed,
And kept from paths which lead unto the dead.
Now this good man has his especial guider,
Then by his going let him know his rider.

Some go as if they did not greatly care,
Whether of heaven or hell they should be heir.
The rein, it seems, is laid upon their neck,
They seem to go their way without a check.
Now this man too has his especial guider,
And by his going he may know his rider.
Some again run as if resolved to die,
Body and soul, to all eternity.
Good counsel they by no means can abide;
They'll have their course whatever them betide.
Now these poor men have their especial guider,
Were they not fools they soon might know their
        rider.
There's one makes head against all godliness,
Those too, that do profess it, he'll distress;
He'll taunt and flout if goodness doth appear,
And at its countenancers mock and jeer.
Now this man, too, has his especial guider,
And by his going he might know his rider.

Bull Run, from 'Horse Latitudes'

While some think there's nothing more rank
than the pool that's long stood aloof
from the freshet, I loved the smell
of sweat and blood and, sí, horse dung
Carlotta shouldered like an Aqua-Lung
as she led me now through that dewy dell
and spread her House of Tartan waterproof.
As we lay there I could have sworn,
as I stared through unruffled thorns
that were an almost perfect fit
to each side of the gravel pit
where she and I'd tried to outflank
each other, I traced the mark of a hoof
(or horseshoe) in her fontanelle.

Astrophil and Stella 41: Having this day my horse, my hand, my lance

Having this day my horse, my hand, my lance
Guided so well that I obtain'd the prize,
Both by the judgment of the English eyes
And of some sent from that sweet enemy France;
Horsemen my skill in horsemanship advance,
Town folks my strength; a daintier judge applies
His praise to sleight which from good use doth rise;
Some lucky wits impute it but to chance;
Others, because of both sides I do take
My blood from them who did excel in this,
Think Nature me a man of arms did make.
How far they shot awry! The true cause is,
Stella look'd on, and from her heav'nly face
Sent forth the beams which made so fair my race.

EAVAN BOLAND

The War Horse

This dry night, nothing unusual
About the clip, clop, casual

Iron of his shoes as he stamps death
Like a mint on the innocent coinage of earth.

I lift the window, watch the ambling feather
Of hock and fetlock, loosed from its daily tether

In the tinker camp on the Enniskerry Road,
Pass, his breath hissing, his snuffling head

Down. He is gone. No great harm is done.
Only a leaf of our laurel hedge is torn—

Of distant interest like a maimed limb,
Only a rose which now will never climb

The stone of our house, expendable, a mere
Line of defence against him, a volunteer

You might say, only a crocus, its bulbous head
Blown from growth, one of the screamless dead.

But we, we are safe, our unformed fear
Of fierce commitment gone; why should we care

If a rose, a hedge, a crocus are uprooted
Like corpses, remote, crushed, mutilated?

He stumbles on like a rumour of war, huge
Threatening. Neighbours use the subterfuge

Of curtains. He stumbles down our short street
Thankfully passing us. I pause, wait,

Then to breathe relief lean on the sill
And for a second only my blood is still

With atavism. That rose he smashed frays
Ribboned across our hedge, recalling days

Of burned countryside, illicit braid:
A cause ruined before, a world betrayed.

Franz Marc's Blue Horses

I step into the painting of the four blue horses.
I am not even surprised that I can do this.
One of the horses walks toward me.
His blue nose noses me lightly. I put my arm
over his blue mane, not holding on, just
    commingling.
He allows me my pleasure.
Franz Marc died a young man, shrapnel in his
    brain.
I would rather die than explain to the blue horses
    what war is.
They would either faint in horror, or simply
    find it impossible to believe.
I do not know how to thank you, Franz Marc.
Maybe our world will grow kinder eventually.
Maybe the desire to make something beautiful
    is the piece of God that is inside each of us.
Now all four horses have come closer,
    are bending their faces toward me
        as if they have secrets to tell.
I don't expect them to speak, and they don't.
If being so beautiful isn't enough, what
    could they possibly say?

Ars Poetica

I wander and wander.
There are paths and there are horses.
There are notebooks and notebooks full of
    handwritten words
where people have wondered their thoughts across
    lines.
Yes, I have been known to make some mistakes.
I have taken myself some places I shouldn't have,
    and I've always been glad.
I shall keep on wandering until I die
although sometimes I feel sick and have to lie down
    for a couple days.
Sometimes I dream of getting tattoos and regretting
    it.
Sometimes sex tricks me into love, and sometimes
    love tricks me into sex,
but I don't mind for long.
My horse looks like a few red streaks someone
    painted in the air.
I'm always surprised when she holds my weight.
Let's kiss goodbye before I climb up and ride on.
I'm grateful to have met you.

from Richard II, Act V, scene V

Enter a Groom of the Stable

Groom
Hail, royal prince!

KING RICHARD II
Thanks, noble peer;
The cheapest of us is ten groats too dear.
What art thou? and how comest thou hither,
Where no man never comes but that sad dog
That brings me food to make misfortune live?

Groom
I was a poor groom of thy stable, king,
When thou wert king; who, travelling towards York,
With much ado at length have gotten leave
To look upon my sometimes royal master's face.
O, how it yearn'd my heart when I beheld
In London streets, that coronation-day,
When Bolingbroke rode on roan Barbary,
That horse that thou so often hast bestrid,
That horse that I so carefully have dress'd!

KING RICHARD II

Rode he on Barbary? Tell me, gentle friend,
How went he under him?

Groom

So proudly as if he disdain'd the ground.

KING RICHARD II

So proud that Bolingbroke was on his back!
That jade hath eat bread from my royal hand;
This hand hath made him proud with clapping him.
Would he not stumble? would he not fall down,
Since pride must have a fall, and break the neck
Of that proud man that did usurp his back?
Forgiveness, horse! why do I rail on thee,
Since thou, created to be awed by man,
Wast born to bear? I was not made a horse;
And yet I bear a burthen like an ass,
Spurr'd, gall'd and tired by jouncing Bolingbroke.

HENRY WADSWORTH LONGFELLOW

Paul Revere's Ride

Listen, my children, and you shall hear
Of the midnight ride of Paul Revere,
On the eighteenth of April, in Seventy-five;
Hardly a man is now alive
Who remembers that famous day and year.

He said to his friend, 'If the British march
By land or sea from the town to-night,
Hang a lantern aloft in the belfry arch
Of the North Church tower, as a signal light,—
One, if by land, and two if by sea;
And I on the opposite shore will be,
Ready to ride and spread the alarm
Through every Middlesex village and farm,
For the country folk to be up and to arm.'
Then he said, 'Good night!' and with muffled oar
Silently rowed to the Charlestown shore,
Just as the moon rose over the bay,
Where swinging wide at her moorings lay
The Somerset, British man-of-war:
A phantom ship, with each mast and spar
Across the moon, like a prison bar,
And a huge black hulk, that was magnified
By its own reflection in the tide.

Meanwhile, his friend, through alley and street
Wanders and watches with eager ears,
Till in the silence around him he hears
The muster of men at the barrack door,
The sound of arms, and the tramp of feet,
And the measured tread of the grenadiers
Marching down to their boats on the shore.

Then he climbed to the tower of the Old North
   Church,
By the wooden stairs, with stealthy tread,
To the belfry-chamber overhead,
And startled the pigeons from their perch
On the sombre rafters, that round him made
Masses and moving shapes of shade,—
By the trembling ladder, steep and tall,
To the highest window in the wall,
Where he paused to listen and look down
A moment on the roofs of the town,
And the moonlight flowing over all.
Beneath, in the churchyard, lay the dead,
In their night-encampment on the hill,
Wrapped in silence so deep and still
That he could hear, like a sentinel's tread,
The watchful night-wind, as it went
Creeping along from tent to tent,
And seeming to whisper, 'All is well!'
A moment only he feels the spell
Of the place and the hour, and the secret dread

Of the lonely belfry and the dead;
For suddenly all his thoughts are bent
On a shadowy something far away,
Where the river widens to meet the bay,—
A line of black, that bends and floats
On the rising tide, like a bridge of boats.

Meanwhile, impatient to mount and ride,
Booted and spurred, with a heavy stride,
On the opposite shore walked Paul Revere.
Now he patted his horse's side,
Now gazed on the landscape far and near,
Then impetuous, stamped the earth,
And turned and tightened his saddle girth;
But mostly he watched with eager search
The belfry-tower of the Old North Church,
As it rose above the graves on the hill,
Lonely and spectral and sombre and still.
And lo! as he looks, on the belfry's height
A glimmer, and then a gleam of light!
He springs to the saddle, the bridle he turns,
But lingers and gazes, till full on his sight
A second lamp in the belfry burns!
A hurry of hoofs in a village-street,
A shape in the moonlight, a bulk in the dark,
And beneath from the pebbles, in passing, a spark
Struck out by a steed flying fearless and fleet:
That was all! And yet, through the gloom and the
    light,

The fate of a nation was riding that night;
And the spark struck out by that steed, in his flight,
Kindled the land into flame with its heat.
He has left the village and mounted the steep,
And beneath him, tranquil and broad and deep,
Is the Mystic, meeting the ocean tides;
And under the alders, that skirt its edge,
Now soft on the sand, now loud on the ledge,
Is heard the tramp of his steed as he rides.

It was twelve by the village clock
When he crossed the bridge into Medford town.
He heard the crowing of the cock,
And the barking of the farmer's dog,
And felt the damp of the river fog,
That rises when the sun goes down.

It was one by the village clock,
When he galloped into Lexington.
He saw the gilded weathercock
Swim in the moonlight as he passed,
And the meeting-house windows, blank and bare,
Gaze at him with a spectral glare,
As if they already stood aghast
At the bloody work they would look upon.

It was two by the village clock,
When be came to the bridge in Concord town.
He heard the bleating of the flock,

And the twitter of birds among the trees,
And felt the breath of the morning breeze
Blowing over the meadows brown.
And one was safe and asleep in his bed
Who at the bridge would be first to fall,
Who that day would be lying dead,
Pierced by a British musket-ball.

You know the rest. In the books you have read,
How the British Regulars fired and fled,—
How the farmers gave them ball for ball,
From behind each fence and farm-yard wall,
Chasing the red-coats down the lane,
Then crossing the fields to emerge again
Under the trees at the turn of the road,
And only pausing to fire and load.

So through the night rode Paul Revere;
And so through the night went his cry of alarm
To every Middlesex village and farm,—
A cry of defiance, and not of fear,
A voice in the darkness, a knock at the door,
And a word that shall echo forevermore!
For, borne on the night-wind of the Past,
Through all our history, to the last,
In the hour of darkness and peril and need,
The people will waken and listen to hear
The hurrying hoof-beats of that steed,
And the midnight message of Paul Revere.

BANJO PATERSON

The Man from Snowy River

There was movement at the station, for the word
    had passed around
That the colt from Old Regret had got away,
And had joined the wild bush horses – he was worth
    a thousand pound,
So all the cracks had gathered to the fray.
All the tried and noted riders from the stations near
    and far
Had mustered at the homestead overnight,
For the bushmen love hard riding where the wild
    bush horses are,
And the stock-horse snuffs the battle with delight.

There was Harrison, who made his pile when
    Pardon won the cup,
The old man with his hair as white as snow;
But few could ride beside him when his blood was
    fairly up –
He would go wherever horse and man could go.
And Clancy of the Overflow came down to lend a
    hand,
No better horseman ever held the reins;
For never horse could throw him while the saddle-
    girths would stand,

He learnt to ride while droving on the plains.

And one was there, a stripling on a small and weedy
    beast;
He was something like a racehorse undersized,
With a touch of Timor pony – three parts
    thoroughbred at least –
And such as are by mountain horsemen prized.
He was hard and tough and wiry – just the sort that
    won't say die –
There was courage in his quick impatient tread;
And he bore the badge of gameness in his bright
    and fiery eye,
And the proud and lofty carriage of his head.

But still so slight and weedy, one would doubt his
    power to stay,
And the old man said, 'That horse will never do
For a long and tiring gallop – lad, you'd better stop
    away,
Those hills are far too rough for such as you.'
So he waited sad and wistful – only Clancy stood his
    friend –
'I think we ought to let him come,' he said;
'I warrant he'll be with us when he's wanted at the
    end,
For both his horse and he are mountain bred.

'He hails from Snowy River, up by Kosciusko's side,

Where the hills are twice as steep and twice as rough;
Where a horse's hoofs strike firelight from the flint
    stones every stride,
The man that holds his own is good enough.
And the Snowy River riders on the mountains make
    their home,
Where the river runs those giant hills between;
I have seen full many horsemen since I first
    commenced to roam,
But nowhere yet such horsemen have I seen.'

So he went; they found the horses by the big
    mimosa clump,
They raced away towards the mountain's brow,
And the old man gave his orders, 'Boys, go at them
    from the jump,
No use to try for fancy riding now.
And, Clancy, you must wheel them, try and wheel
    them to the right.
Ride boldly, lad, and never fear the spills,
For never yet was rider that could keep the mob in
    sight,
If once they gain the shelter of those hills.'

So Clancy rode to wheel them – he was racing on
    the wing
Where the best and boldest riders take their place,
And he raced his stockhorse past them, and he
    made the ranges ring

With the stockwhip, as he met them face to face.
Then they halted for a moment, while he swung the
    dreaded lash,
But they saw their well-loved mountain full in view,
And they charged beneath the stockwhip with a
    sharp and sudden dash,
And off into the mountain scrub they flew.

Then fast the horsemen followed, where the gorges
    deep and black
Resounded to the thunder of their tread,
And the stockwhips woke the echoes, and they
    fiercely answered back
From cliffs and crags that beetled overhead.
And upward, ever upward, the wild horses held
    their way,
Where Mountain Ash and Kurrajong grew wide;
And the old man muttered fiercely, 'We may bid the
    mob good day,
No man can hold them down the other side.'

When they reached the mountain's summit, even
    Clancy took a pull –
It well might make the boldest hold their breath;
The wild hop scrub grew thickly, and the hidden
    ground was full
Of wombat holes, and any slip was death.
But the man from Snowy River let the pony have his
    head,

And he swung his stockwhip round and gave a cheer,
And he raced him down the mountain like a torrent
down its bed,
While the others stood and watched in very fear.

He sent the flint-stones flying, but the pony kept his
feet,
He cleared the fallen timbers in his stride,
And the man from Snowy River never shifted in his
seat —
It was grand to see that mountain horseman ride.
Through the stringy barks and saplings, on the
rough and broken ground,
Down the hillside at a racing pace he went;
And he never drew the bridle till he landed safe and
sound
At the bottom of that terrible descent.

He was right among the horses as they climbed the
farther hill,
And the watchers on the mountain standing mute,
Saw him ply the stockwhip fiercely; he was right
among them still,
As he raced across the clearing in pursuit.
Then they lost him for a moment, where two
mountain gullies met
In the ranges — but a final glimpse reveals
On a dim and distant hillside the wild horses racing
yet,

With the man from Snowy River at their heels.

And he ran them single-handed till their sides were
    white with foam;
He followed like a bloodhound on their track,
Till they halted cowed and beaten; then he turned
    their heads for home,
And alone and unassisted brought them back.
But his hardy mountain pony he could scarcely raise
    a trot,
He was blood from hip to shoulder from the spur;
But his pluck was still undaunted, and his courage
    fiery hot,
For never yet was mountain horse a cur.

And down by Kosciusko, where the pine-clad ridges
    raise
Their torn and rugged battlements on high,
Where the air is clear as crystal, and the white stars
    fairly blaze
At midnight in the cold and frosty sky,
And where around the Overflow the reed-beds
    sweep and sway
To the breezes, and the rolling plains are wide,
The man from Snowy River is a household word
    today,
And the stockmen tell the story of his ride.

JANE HIRSHFIELD

Heat

My mare, when she was in heat,
would travel the fenceline for hours,
wearing the impatience
in her feet into the ground.

Not a stallion for miles, I'd assure her,
give it up.

She'd widen her nostrils,
sieve the wind for news, be moving again,
her underbelly darkening with sweat,
then stop at the gate a moment, wait
to see what I might do.
Oh, I knew
how it was for her, easily
recognized myself in that wide lust:
came to stand in the pasture
just to see it played.
Offered a hand, a bucket of grain—
a minute's distraction from passion
the most I gave.

Then she'd return to what burned her:

the fence, the fence,
so hoping I might see, might let her free.
I'd envy her then,
to be so restlessly sure
of heat, and need, and what it takes
to feed the wanting that we are—

only a gap to open
the width of a mare,
the rest would take care of itself.
Surely, surely I knew that,
who had the power of bucket
and bridle—
she would beseech me, sidle up,
be gone, as life is short.
But desire, desire is long.

SEAMUS HEANEY

Follower

My father worked with a horse-plough,
His shoulders globed like a full sail strung
Between the shafts and the furrow.
The horses strained at his clicking tongue.

An expert. He would set the wing
And fit the bright steel-pointed sock.
The sod rolled over without breaking.
At the headrig, with a single pluck

Of reins, the sweating team turned round
And back into the land. His eye
Narrowed and angled at the ground,
Mapping the furrow exactly.

I stumbled in his hobnailed wake,
Fell sometimes on the polished sod;
Sometimes he rode me on his back
Dipping and rising to his plod.

I wanted to grow up and plough,
To close one eye, stiffen my arm.
All I ever did was follow

In his broad shadow round the farm.

I was a nuisance, tripping, falling,
Yapping always. But today
It is my father who keeps stumbling
Behind me, and will not go away

White Horses

Where run your colts at pasture?
  Where hide your mares to breed?
'Mid bergs about the Ice-cap
  Or wove Sargasso weed;
By chartless reef and channel,
  Or crafty coastwise bars,
But most the ocean-meadows
  All purple to the stars!

Who holds the rein upon you?
  The latest gale let free.
What meat is in your mangers?
  The glut of all the sea.
'Twixt tide and tide's returning
  Great store of newly dead, —
The bones of those that faced us,
  And the hearts of those that fled.
Afar, off-shore and single,
  Some stallion, rearing swift,
Neighs hungry for new fodder,
  And calls us to the drift:
Then down the cloven ridges —
  A million hooves unshod —

Break forth the mad White Horses
  To seek their meat from God!

Girth-deep in hissing water
  Our furious vanguard strains —
Through mist of mighty tramplings
  Roll up the fore-blown manes —
A hundred leagues to leeward,
  Ere yet the deep is stirred,
The groaning rollers carry
  The coming of the herd!

Whose hand may grip your nostrils —
  Your forelock who may hold?
E'en they that use the broads with us —
  The riders bred and bold,
That spy upon our matings,
  That rope us where we run —
They know the strong White Horses
  From father unto son.

We breathe about their cradles,
  We race their babes ashore,
We snuff against their thresholds,
  We nuzzle at their door;
By day with stamping squadrons,
  By night in whinnying droves,
Creep up the wise White Horses,
  To call them from their loves.

And come they for your calling?
  No wit of man may save.
They hear the loosed White Horses
  Above their fathers' grave;
And, kin of those we crippled,
  And, sons of those we slew,
Spur down the wild white riders
  To school the herds anew.

What service have ye paid them,
  Oh jealous steeds and strong?
Save we that throw their weaklings,
  Is none dare work them wrong;
While thick around the homestead
  Our snow-backed leaders graze —
A guard behind their plunder,
  And a veil before their ways.

With march and countermarchings —
  With weight of wheeling hosts —
Stray mob or bands embattled —
  We ring the chosen coasts:
And, careless of our clamour
  That bids the stranger fly,
At peace with our pickets
  The wild white riders lie.

. . . .

Trust ye that curdled hollows —
  Trust ye the neighing wind —
Trust ye the moaning groundswell —
  Our herds are close behind!
To bray your foeman's armies —
  To chill and snap his sword —
Trust ye the wild White Horses,
  The Horses of the Lord!

I Love Them As I'm Defying Them

I am the new colt.
I took the creamery road to the palace.
I took the chill-knob to be polished.
It was a lonely way.

My underside is beige and surprising
as the belly of a fire truck.
I took the creamery road.
I took the palace.

Tearing the grass with my black feet
I struck at the night with my firetruck neck
and found it once, the palace.

I am in it now alone.
I am precious like rosacea.
I stand for youth on my new knees
and I carried this flag the whole way.

I am several.
I am not harmless. I am small horses.

ALFRED LORD TENNYSON

from 'Eric and Enide, Idylls of the King'

And Enid answered, 'Yea, my lord, I know
Your wish, and would obey; but riding first,
I hear the violent threats you do not hear,
I see the danger which you cannot see:
Then not to give you warning, that seems hard;
Almost beyond me: yet I would obey.'

 'Yea so,' said he, 'do it: be not too wise;
Seeing that ye are wedded to a man,
Not all mismated with a yawning clown,
But one with arms to guard his head and yours,
With eyes to find you out however far,
And ears to hear you even in his dreams.'

 With that he turned and looked as keenly at her
As careful robins eye the delver's toil;
And that within her, which a wanton fool,
Or hasty judger would have called her guilt,
Made her cheek burn and either eyelid fall.
And Geraint looked and was not satisfied.

 Then forward by a way which, beaten broad,

Led from the territory of false Limours
To the waste earldom of another earl,
Doorm, whom his shaking vassals called the Bull,
Went Enid with her sullen follower on.
Once she looked back, and when she saw him ride
More near by many a rood than yestermorn,
It wellnigh made her cheerful; till Geraint
Waving an angry hand as who should say
'Ye watch me,' saddened all her heart again.
But while the sun yet beat a dewy blade,
The sound of many a heavily-galloping hoof
Smote on her ear, and turning round she saw
Dust, and the points of lances bicker in it.
Then not to disobey her lord's behest,
And yet to give him warning, for he rode
As if he heard not, moving back she held
Her finger up, and pointed to the dust.
At which the warrior in his obstinacy,
Because she kept the letter of his word,
Was in a manner pleased, and turning, stood.
And in the moment after, wild Limours,
Borne on a black horse, like a thunder-cloud
Whose skirts are loosened by the breaking storm,
Half ridden off with by the thing he rode,
And all in passion uttering a dry shriek,
Dashed on Geraint, who closed with him, and bore
Down by the length of lance and arm beyond
The crupper, and so left him stunned or dead,
And overthrew the next that followed him,

And blindly rushed on all the rout behind.
But at the flash and motion of the man
They vanished panic-stricken, like a shoal
Of darting fish, that on a summer morn
Adown the crystal dykes at Camelot
Come slipping o'er their shadows on the sand,
But if a man who stands upon the brink
But lift a shining hand against the sun,
There is not left the twinkle of a fin
Betwixt the cressy islets white in flower;
So, scared but at the motion of the man,
Fled all the boon companions of the Earl,
And left him lying in the public way;
So vanish friendships only made in wine.

Then like a stormy sunlight smiled Geraint,
Who saw the chargers of the two that fell
Start from their fallen lords, and wildly fly,
Mixt with the flyers. 'Horse and man,' he said,
'All of one mind and all right-honest friends!
Not a hoof left: and I methinks till now
Was honest—paid with horses and with arms;
I cannot steal or plunder, no nor beg:
And so what say ye, shall we strip him there
Your lover? has your palfrey heart enough
To bear his armour? shall we fast, or dine?
No?—then do thou, being right honest, pray
That we may meet the horsemen of Earl Doorm,
I too would still be honest.' Thus he said:

And sadly gazing on her bridle-reins,
And answering not one word, she led the way.

  But as a man to whom a dreadful loss
Falls in a far land and he knows it not,
But coming back he learns it, and the loss
So pains him that he sickens nigh to death;
So fared it with Geraint, who being pricked
In combat with the follower of Limours,
Bled underneath his armour secretly,
And so rode on, nor told his gentle wife
What ailed him, hardly knowing it himself,
Till his eye darkened and his helmet wagged;
And at a sudden swerving of the road,
Though happily down on a bank of grass,
The Prince, without a word, from his horse fell.

  And Enid heard the clashing of his fall,
Suddenly came, and at his side all pale
Dismounting, loosed the fastenings of his arms,
Nor let her true hand falter, nor blue eye
Moisten, till she had lighted on his wound,
And tearing off her veil of faded silk
Had bared her forehead to the blistering sun,
And swathed the hurt that drained her dear lord's
    life.
Then after all was done that hand could do,
She rested, and her desolation came
Upon her, and she wept beside the way.

And many past, but none regarded her,
For in that realm of lawless turbulence,
A woman weeping for her murdered mate
Was cared as much for as a summer shower:
One took him for a victim of Earl Doorm,
Nor dared to waste a perilous pity on him:
Another hurrying past, a man-at-arms,
Rode on a mission to the bandit Earl;
Half whistling and half singing a coarse song,
He drove the dust against her veilless eyes:
Another, flying from the wrath of Doorm
Before an ever-fancied arrow, made
The long way smoke beneath him in his fear;
At which her palfrey whinnying lifted heel,
And scoured into the coppices and was lost,
While the great charger stood, grieved like a man.

But at the point of noon the huge Earl Doorm,
Broad-faced with under-fringe of russet beard,
Bound on a foray, rolling eyes of prey,
Came riding with a hundred lances up;
But ere he came, like one that hails a ship,
Cried out with a big voice, 'What, is he dead?'
'No, no, not dead!' she answered in all haste.
'Would some of your kind people take him up,
And bear him hence out of this cruel sun?
Most sure am I, quite sure, he is not dead.'

Then said Earl Doorm: 'Well, if he be not dead,

Why wail ye for him thus? ye seem a child.
And be he dead, I count you for a fool;
Your wailing will not quicken him: dead or not,
Ye mar a comely face with idiot tears.
Yet, since the face is comely—some of you,
Here, take him up, and bear him to our hall:
An if he live, we will have him of our band;
And if he die, why earth has earth enough
To hide him. See ye take the charger too,
A noble one.'

JENNIFER GROTZ

The Ocracoke Ponies

No one saw the first ones
swim ashore centuries ago,
nudged by waves into the marsh grasses.

When you look into their faces, there is no trace
of the ship seized with terror, the crashing waves
and the horses' cries when thrown overboard.

Every afternoon you ride your bicycle to the pasture
to watch the twitch of their manes and ivory tails
unroll a carpet of silence, to see ponies lost in
    dream.

But it isn't dream, that place
your mind drifts to, that museum of memory
inventoried in opposition to the present.

You felt it once on a plane,
taking off from a city you didn't want to leave,
the stranded moment when the plane lifts into the
    clouds.

That's not dream, it's not even sleeping.

It is the nature of sleeping to be unaware.
This was some kind of waiting for the world to
   come back.

ROBERT BROWNING

Boot and Saddle

Boot, saddle, to horse, and away!
Rescue my Castle, before the hot day
Brightens the blue from its silvery grey,

(Chorus) 'Boot, saddle, to horse, and away!'

Ride past the suburbs, asleep as you'd say;
Many's the friend there, will listen and pray
'God's luck to gallants that strike up the lay,

(Chorus) Boot, saddle, to horse, and away!'

Forty miles off, like a roebuck at bay,
Flouts Castle Brancepeth the Roundheads' array:
Who laughs, 'Good fellows ere this, by my fay,

(Chorus) Boot, saddle, to horse, and away!'

Who? My wife Gertrude; that, honest and gay,
Laughs when you talk of surrendering, 'Nay!
I've better counsellors; what counsel they?'

(Chorus) 'Boot, saddle, to horse, and away!'

EDWIN MUIR

The Horses

Barely a twelvemonth after
The seven days war that put the world to sleep,
Late in the evening the strange horses came.
By then we had made our covenant with silence,
But in the first few days it was so still

We listened to our breathing and were afraid.
On the second day
The radios failed; we turned the knobs; no answer.
On the third day a warship passed us, heading north,
Dead bodies piled on the deck. On the sixth day

A plane plunged over us into the sea. Thereafter
Nothing. The radios dumb;
And still they stand in corners of our kitchens,
And stand, perhaps, turned on, in a million rooms
All over the world. But now if they should speak,

If on a sudden they should speak again,
If on the stroke of noon a voice should speak,
We would not listen, we would not let it bring
That old bad world that swallowed its children
    quick

At one great gulp. We would not have it again.

Sometimes we think of the nations lying asleep,
Curled blindly in impenetrable sorrow,
And then the thought confounds us with its
    strangeness.
The tractors lie about our fields; at evening
They look like dank sea-monsters couched and
    waiting.

We leave them where they are and let them rust:
'They'll molder away and be like other loam.'
We make our oxen drag our rusty plows,
Long laid aside. We have gone back
Far past our fathers' land.

And then, that evening
Late in the summer the strange horses came.
We heard a distant tapping on the road,
A deepening drumming; it stopped, went on again
And at the corner changed to hollow thunder.
We saw the heads

Like a wild wave charging and were afraid.
We had sold our horses in our fathers' time
To buy new tractors. Now they were strange to us
As fabulous steeds set on an ancient shield.
Or illustrations in a book of knights.

We did not dare go near them. Yet they waited,
Stubborn and shy, as if they had been sent
By an old command to find our whereabouts
And that long-lost archaic companionship.
In the first moment we had never a thought

That they were creatures to be owned and used.
Among them were some half a dozen colts
Dropped in some wilderness of the broken world,
Yet new as if they had come from their own Eden.
Since then they have pulled our plows and borne
    our loads

But that free servitude still can pierce our hearts.
Our life is changed; their coming our beginning.

THE PEARL POET
Translated by AS Kline

from 'Sir Gawain and the Green Knight'

Then was Gringolet readied, that was huge and
    great,
and had been stabled snugly and in secure wise;
he was eager to gallop, that proud horse then.
The knight went to him and gazed at his coat,
and said soberly to himself, and swore by the truth:
'Here are many, in this motte, that of honour think.
The man who maintains it, joy may he have!
The fair lady through life may love her befall!
Thus if they for charity cherish a guest,
and hold honour in their hand, the Lord them
    reward
who upholds the heavens on high, and also you all!
And if I should live for any while upon earth,
I would grant you some reward readily, if I might.'
Then steps he into the stirrup and strides aloft.
His man showed him his shield; on shoulder he
    slung it,
gives spur to Gringolet with his gilded heels,
and he starts forth on the stones – pausing no
    longer

to prance.
His servant to horse got then,
who bore his spear and lance.
'This castle to Christ I commend:
May he grant it good chance!'

ADAM LINDSAY GORDON

from 'Ye Wearie Wayfarer'

Hark! the bells of distant cattle
Waft across the range,
Through the golden-tufted wattle
Music low and strange;
Like the marriage of peal fairies
Comes the tinkling sound,
Or like chimes of sweet St Mary's
On far English ground.
How my courser champs the snaffle,
And with nostrils spread,
Snorts and scarcely seems to ruffle
Fern leaves with his tread;
Cool and pleasant on his haunches
Blows the evening breeze,
Through the overhanging branches
Of the wattle trees;

Onward! to the Southern Ocean
Glides the breath of Spring.
Onward! with a dreamy motion,
I, too, glide and sing
Forward! forward! still we wander
Tinted hills that lie

In the red horizon yonder
Is the goal so nigh?

Whisper, spring wind, softly singing,
Whisper in my ear;
Respite and nepenthe bringing,
Can the goal be near?
Laden with the dew of vespers,
From the fragrant sky,
In my ear the wind that wispers
Seems to make reply
'Question not, but live and labour
'Til yon goal be won,
Helping every feeble neighbour,
Seeking help from none;
Life is mostly froth and bubble,
Two things stand like stone,
Kindness in another's trouble,
Courage in your own.'

Mare and Newborn Foal

When you die
there are bales of hay
heaped high in space
mean while
with my tongue
I draw the black straw
out of you
mean while
with your tongue
you draw the black straw out of me.

SIR PHILIP SIDNEY

Astrophil and Stella 49: I on my horse, and Love on me, doth try

I on my horse, and Love on me, doth try
Our horsemanships, while by strange work I prove
A horseman to my horse, a horse to Love,
And now man's wrongs in me, poor beast, descry.
The reins wherewith my rider doth me tie
Are humbled thoughts, which bit of reverence
    move,
Curbed in with fear, but with gilt boss above
Of hope, which makes it seem fair to the eye.
The wand is will; thou, fancy, saddle art,
Girt fast by memory; and while I spur
My horse, he spurs with sharp desire to my heart;
He sits me fast, however I do stir;
And now hath made me to his hand so right
That in the manage myself takes delight.

PAISLEY REKDAL

Why Some Girls Love Horses

And then I thought, Can I have more
of this, would it be possible
for every day to be a greater awakening: more light,
more light, your face on the pillow
with the sleep creases rudely
fragmenting it, hair so stiff
from paint and sheet rock it feels
like the dirty short hank
of mane I used to grab on Dandy's neck
before he hauled me up and forward,
white flanks flecked green
with shit and the satin of his dander,
the livingness, the warmth
of all that blood just under the skin
and in the long, thick muscle of the neck—
He was smarter than most of the children
I went to school with. He knew
how to stand with just the crescent
of his hoof along a boot toe and press,
incrementally, his whole weight down. The pain
so surprising when it came,
its iron intention sheathed in stealth, the decisive
sudden twisting of his leg until the hoof

pinned one's foot completely to the ground,
we'd have to beat and beat him with a brush
to push him off, that hot
insistence with its large horse eye trained
deliberately on us, to watch—

Like us, he knew how to announce through violence
how he didn't hunger, didn't want
despite our practiced ministrations: too young
not to try to empathize
with this cunning: this thing
that was and was not human we must respect
for itself and not our imagination of it: I loved him
    because
I could not love him anymore
in the ways I'd taught myself,
watching the slim bodies of teenagers
guide their geldings in figure eights around the ring
as if they were one body, one fluid motion
of electric understanding I would never feel
working its way through fingers to the bit: this
    thing
had a name, a need, a personality; it possessed
an indifference that gave me
logic and a measure: I too might stop wanting
the hand placed on back or shoulder
and never feel the desired response.
I loved the horse for the pain it could imagine

and inflict on me, the sudden jerking
of head away from halter, the tentative nose
inspecting first before it might decide
to relent and eat. I loved
what was not slave or instinct, that when you turn
    to me
it is a choice, it is always a choice to imagine
    pleasure
might be blended, one warmth
bleeding into another as the future
bleeds into the past, more light, more light,
your hand against my shoulder, the image
of the one who taught me disobedience
is the first right of being alive.

ROBERT FROST

Stopping by Woods on a Snowy Evening

Whose woods these are I think I know.
His house is in the village though;
He will not see me stopping here
To watch his woods fill up with snow.

My little horse must think it queer
To stop without a farmhouse near
Between the woods and frozen lake
The darkest evening of the year.

He gives his harness bells a shake
To ask if there is some mistake.
The only other sound's the sweep
Of easy wind and downy flake.

The woods are lovely, dark and deep,
But I have promises to keep,
And miles to go before I sleep,
And miles to go before I sleep.

LORD BYRON

from 'Mazeppa'

IX.
'"Bring forth the horse!"—the horse was brought;
In truth, he was a noble steed,
A Tartar of the Ukraine breed,
Who looked as though the speed of thought
Were in his limbs; but he was wild,
Wild as the wild deer, and untaught,
With spur and bridle undefiled—
'Twas but a day he had been caught;
And snorting, with erected mane,
And struggling fiercely, but in vain,
In the full foam of wrath and dread
To me the desert-born was led:
They bound me on, that menial throng,
Upon his back with many a thong;
They loosed him with a sudden lash—
Away!—away!—and on we dash!—
Torrents less rapid and less rash.

X.
'Away!—away!—my breath was gone—
I saw not where he hurried on:
'Twas scarcely yet the break of day,

And on he foamed—away!—away!—
The last of human sounds which rose,
As I was darted from my foes,
Was the wild shout of savage laughter,
Which on the wind came roaring after
A moment from that rabble rout:
With sudden wrath I wrenched my head,
And snapped the cord, which to the mane
Had bound my neck in lieu of rein,
And, writhing half my form about,
Howled back my curse; but 'midst the tread,
The thunder of my courser's speed,
Perchance they did not hear nor heed:
It vexes me—for I would fain
Have paid their insult back again.
I paid it well in after days:
There is not of that castle gate.
Its drawbridge and portcullis' weight,
Stone, bar, moat, bridge, or barrier left;
Nor of its fields a blade of grass,
Save what grows on a ridge of wall,
Where stood the hearth-stone of the hall;
And many a time ye there might pass,
Nor dream that e'er the fortress was.
I saw its turrets in a blaze,
Their crackling battlements all cleft,
And the hot lead pour down like rain
From off the scorched and blackening roof,
Whose thickness was not vengeance-proof.

They little thought that day of pain,
When launched, as on the lightning's flash,
They bade me to destruction dash,
That one day I should come again,
With twice five thousand horse, to thank
The Count for his uncourteous ride.
They played me then a bitter prank,
When, with the wild horse for my guide,
They bound me to his foaming flank:
At length I played them one as frank—
For time at last sets all things even—
And if we do but watch the hour,
There never yet was human power
Which could evade, if unforgiven,
The patient search and vigil long
Of him who treasures up a wrong.

XI.
'Away, away, my steed and I,
Upon the pinions of the wind.
All human dwellings left behind,
We sped like meteors through the sky,
When with its crackling sound the night
Is chequered with the northern light:
Town—village—none were on our track,
But a wild plain of far extent,
And bounded by a forest black;
And, save the scarce seen battlement
On distant heights of some strong hold,

Against the Tartars built of old,
No trace of man. The year before
A Turkish army had marched o'er;
And where the Spahi's hoof hath trod,
The verdure flies the bloody sod:—
The sky was dull, and dim, and grey,
And a low breeze crept moaning by—
I could have answered with a sigh—
But fast we fled, away, away—
And I could neither sigh nor pray—
And my cold sweat-drops fell like rain
Upon the courser's bristling mane;
But, snorting still with rage and fear,
He flew upon his far career:
At times I almost thought, indeed,
He must have slackened in his speed;
But no—my bound and slender frame
Was nothing to his angry might,
And merely like a spur became:
Each motion which I made to free
My swoln limbs from their agony
Increased his fury and affright:
I tried my voice,—'twas faint and low,
But yet he swerved as from a blow;
And, starting to each accent, sprang
As from a sudden trumpet's clang:
Meantime my cords were wet with gore,
Which, oozing through my limbs, ran o'er;
And in my tongue the thirst became
A something fierier far than flame.

XII.

'We neared the wild wood—'twas so wide,
I saw no bounds on either side;
'Twas studded with old sturdy trees,
That bent not to the roughest breeze
Which howls down from Siberia's waste,
And strips the forest in its haste,—
But these were few and far between,
Set thick with shrubs more young and green,
Luxuriant with their annual leaves,
Ere strown by those autumnal eves
That nip the forest's foliage dead,
Discoloured with a lifeless red,
Which stands thereon like stiffened gore
Upon the slain when battle's o'er,
And some long winter's night hath shed
Its frost o'er every tombless head,
So cold and stark, the raven's beak
May peck unpierced each frozen cheek:
'Twas a wild waste of underwood,
And here and there a chestnut stood,
The strong oak, and the hardy pine;
But far apart—and well it were,
Or else a different lot were mine—
The boughs gave way, and did not tear
My limbs; and I found strength to bear
My wounds, already scarred with cold—
My bonds forbade to loose my hold.
We rustled through the leaves like wind,

Left shrubs, and trees, and wolves behind;
By night I heard them on the track,
Their troop came hard upon our back,
With their long gallop, which can tire
The hound's deep hate, and hunter's fire:
Where'er we flew they followed on,
Nor left us with the morning sun;
Behind I saw them, scarce a rood,
At day-break winding through the wood,
And through the night had heard their feet
Their stealing, rustling step repeat.
Oh! how I wished for spear or sword,
At least to die amidst the horde,
And perish—if it must be so—
At bay, destroying many a foe
When first my courser's race begun,
I wished the goal already won;
But now I doubted strength and speed:
Vain doubt! his swift and savage breed
Had nerved him like the mountain-roe;
Nor faster falls the blinding snow
Which whelms the peasant near the door
Whose threshold he shall cross no more,
Bewildered with the dazzling blast,
Than through the forest-paths he passed—
Untired, untamed, and worse than wild;
All furious as a favoured child
Balked of its wish; or fiercer still,
A woman piqued—who has her will.

XIII.

'The wood was passed; 'twas more than noon,
But chill the air, although in June;
Or it might be my veins ran cold—
Prolonged endurance tames the bold;
And I was then not what I seem,
But headlong as a wintry stream,
And wore my feelings out before
I well could count their causes o'er:
And what with fury, fear, and wrath,
The tortures which beset my path,
Cold, hunger, sorrow, shame, distress,
Thus bound in nature's nakedness;
Sprung from a race whose rising blood
When stirred beyond its calmer mood,
And trodden hard upon, is like
The rattle-snake's, in act to strike,
What marvel if this worn-out trunk
Beneath its woes a moment sunk?
The earth gave way, the skies rolled round,
I seemed to sink upon the ground;
But erred, for I was fastly bound.
My heart turned sick, my brain grew sore,
And throbbed awhile, then beat no more:
The skies spun like a mighty wheel;
I saw the trees like drunkards reel,
And a slight flash sprang o'er my eyes,
Which saw no farther. He who dies
Can die no more than then I died;

O'ertortured by that ghastly ride,
I felt the blackness come and go,
And strove to wake; but could not make
My senses climb up from below:
I felt as on a plank at sea,
When all the waves that dash o'er thee,
At the same time upheave and whelm,
And hurl thee towards a desert realm.
My undulating life was as
The fancied lights that flitting pass
Our shut eyes in deep midnight, when
Fever begins upon the brain;
But soon it passed, with little pain,
But a confusion worse than such:
I own that I should deem it much,
Dying, to feel the same again;
And yet I do suppose we must
Feel far more ere we turn to dust:
No matter; I have bared my brow
Full in Death's face—before—and now.

XIV.
'My thoughts came back; where was I? Cold,
And numb, and giddy: pulse by pulse
Life reassumed its lingering hold,
And throb by throb—till grown a pang;
Which for a moment would convulse,
My blood reflowed, though thick and chill;
My ear with uncouth noises rang,

My heart began once more to thrill;
My sight returned, though dim; alas!
And thickened, as it were, with glass.
Methought the dash of waves was nigh;
There was a gleam too of the sky
Studded with stars;—it is no dream;
The wild horse swims the wilder stream!
The bright broad river's gushing tide
Sweeps, winding onward, far and wide,
And we are half-way, struggling o'er
To yon unknown and silent shore.
The waters broke my hollow trance,
And with a temporary strength
My stiffened limbs were rebaptized.
My courser's broad breast proudly braves,
And dashes off the ascending waves,
And onward we advance
We reach the slippery shore at length,
A haven I but little prized,
For all behind was dark and drear,
And all before was night and fear.
How many hours of night or day
In those suspended pangs I lay,
I could not tell; I scarcely knew
If this were human breath I drew.

XV.
'With glossy skin, and dripping mane,
And reeling limbs, and reeking flank,

The wild steed's sinewy nerves still strain
Up the repelling bank.
We gain the top: a boundless plain
Spreads through the shadow of the night,
And onward, onward, onward, seems,
Like precipices in our dreams,
To stretch beyond the sight;
And here and there a speck of white,
Or scattered spot of dusky green,
In masses broke into the light,
As rose the moon upon my right:
But nought distinctly seen
In the dim waste would indicate
The omen of a cottage gate;
No twinkling taper from afar
Stood like a hospitable star;
Not even an ignis-fatuus rose
To make him merry with my woes:
That very cheat had cheered me then!
Although detected, welcome still,
Reminding me, through every ill,
Of the abodes of men.

XVI.
'Onward we went—but slack and slow
His savage force at length o'erspent,
The drooping courser, faint and low,
All feebly foaming went.
A sickly infant had had power

To guide him forward in that hour!
But, useless all to me,
His new-born tameness nought availed—
My limbs were bound; my force had failed,
Perchance, had they been free.
With feeble effort still I tried
To rend the bonds so starkly tied,
But still it was in vain;
My limbs were only wrung the more,
And soon the idle strife gave o'er,
Which but prolonged their pain:
The dizzy race seemed almost done,
Although no goal was nearly won.
Some streaks announced the coming sun—
How slow, alas! he came!
Methought that mist of dawning grey
Would never dapple into day;
How heavily it rolled away—
Before the eastern flame
Rose crimson, and deposed the stars,
And called the radiance from their cars,
And filled the earth, from his deep throne,
With lonely lustre, all his own.

XVII.
'Up rose the sun; the mists were curled
Back from the solitary world
Which lay around—behind—before;
What booted it to traverse o'er

Plain, forest, river? Man nor brute,
Nor dint of hoof, nor print of foot,
Lay in the wild luxuriant soil;
No sign of travel—none of toil;
The very air was mute:
And not an insect's shrill small horn,
Nor matin bird's new voice was borne
From herb nor thicket. Many a werst,
Panting as if his heart would burst,
The weary brute still staggered on;
And still we were—or seemed—alone:
At length, while reeling on our way,
Methought I heard a courser neigh,
From out yon tuft of blackening firs.
Is it the wind those branches stirs?
No, no! from out the forest prance
A trampling troop; I see them come!
In one vast squadron they advance!
I strove to cry—my lips were dumb.
The steeds rush on in plunging pride;
But where are they the reins to guide?
A thousand horse—and none to ride!
With flowing tail, and flying mane,
Wide nostrils never stretched by pain,
Mouths bloodless to the bit or rein,
And feet that iron never shod,
And flanks unscarred by spur or rod,
A thousand horse, the wild, the free,
Like waves that follow o'er the sea,

Came thickly thundering on,
As if our faint approach to meet;
The sight re-nerved my courser's feet,
A moment staggering, feebly fleet,
A moment, with a faint low neigh,
He answered, and then fell!
With gasps and glazing eyes he lay,
And reeking limbs immoveable,
His first and last career is done!
On came the troop—they saw him stoop,
They saw me strangely bound along
His back with many a bloody thong.
They stop—they start—they snuff the air,
Gallop a moment here and there,
Approach, retire, wheel round and round,
Then plunging back with sudden bound,
Headed by one black mighty steed,
Who seemed the patriarch of his breed,
Without a single speck or hair
Of white upon his shaggy hide;
They snort—they foam—neigh—swerve aside,
And backward to the forest fly,
By instinct, from a human eye.
They left me there to my despair,
Linked to the dead and stiffening wretch,
Whose lifeless limbs beneath me stretch,
Relieved from that unwonted weight,
From whence I could not extricate
Nor him nor me—and there we lay

The dying on the dead!
I little deemed another day
Would see my houseless, helpless head.

'And there from morn till twilight bound,
I felt the heavy hours toil round,
With just enough of life to see
My last of suns go down on me,
In hopeless certainty of mind,
That makes us feel at length resigned
To that which our foreboding years
Presents the worst and last of fears
Inevitable—even a boon,
Nor more unkind for coming soon,
Yet shunned and dreaded with such care,
As if it only were a snare
That prudence might escape:
At times both wished for and implored,
At times sought with self-pointed sword,
Yet still a dark and hideous close
To even intolerable woes,
And welcome in no shape.
And, strange to say, the sons of pleasure,
They who have revelled beyond measure
In beauty, wassail, wine, and treasure,
Die calm, or calmer, oft than he
Whose heritage was misery.
For he who hath in turn run through
All that was beautiful and new,

Hath nought to hope, and nought to leave;
And, save the future, (which is viewed
Not quite as men are base or good,
But as their nerves may be endued,)
With nought perhaps to grieve:
The wretch still hopes his woes must end,
And death, whom he should deem his friend,
Appears, to his distempered eyes,
Arrived to rob him of his prize,
The tree of his new Paradise.
Tomorrow would have given him all,
Repaid his pangs, repaired his fall;
Tomorrow would have been the first
Of days no more deplored or curst,
But bright, and long, and beckoning years,
Seen dazzling through the mist of tears,
Guerdon of many a painful hour;
Tomorrow would have given him power
To rule, to shine, to smite, to save—
And must it dawn upon his grave?

JANE COMMANE

Seven Horse Secrets

The horse's heart is a grand mansion of four piston-
     firing chambers.
A horse sees a world blurred in the two-tone
     flourish of the photo finish.
Look into the amber planet of a horse's eye and a
     refracted universe forms there.
Horses turn the turf of an ever-moving, never-quite-
     touched earth beneath their hooves.
Horses laugh at our expense; lips peeled, ivory-
     gravestone teeth bared, domino pieces unplaced.
Horses are melancholic humourists; they know of
     the pending darkness beyond the five-bar gate,
     beyond the green paddock. Hancock learned all
     he knew from horses.
Horses tramp the ancient treadmill of our whims,
     trot to our biding, broken, bought and sold,
     but only ever possess themselves.

The Horses

I climbed through woods in the hour-before-dawn
    dark.
Evil air, a frost-making stillness,

Not a leaf, not a bird –
A world cast in frost. I came out above the wood

Where my breath left tortuous statues in the iron
    light.
But the valleys were draining the darkness

Till the moorline – blackening dregs of the
    brightening grey –
Halved the sky ahead. And I saw the horses:

Huge in the dense grey – ten together –
Megalith-still. They breathed, making no move,

With draped manes and tilted hind-hooves,
Making no sound.

I passed: not one snorted or jerked its head.
Grey silent fragments

Of a grey still world.

I listened in emptiness on the moor-ridge.
The curlew's tear turned its edge on the silence.

Slowly detail leafed from the darkness. Then the
    sun
Orange, red, red erupted

Silently, and splitting to its core tore and flung
    cloud,
Shook the gulf open, showed blue,

And the big planets hanging –
I turned

Stumbling in a fever of a dream, down towards
The dark woods, from the kindling tops,

And came the horses.
                                There, still they stood,
But now steaming, and glistening under the flow of
    light,

Their draped stone manes, their tilted hind-hooves
Stirring under a thaw while all around them

The frost showed its fires. But still they made no
    sound.

Not one snorted or stamped,

Their hung heads patient as the horizons,
High over valleys, in the red levelling rays –

In din of the crowded streets, going among the
    years, the faces,
May I still meet my memory in so lonely a place

Between the streams and the red clouds, hearing
    curlews,
Hearing the horizons endure.

The Old Whim Horse

He's an old grey horse, with his head bowed sadly,
  And with dim old eyes and a queer roll aft,
With the off-fore sprung and the hind screwed
    badly,
  And he bears all over the brands of graft;
And he lifts his head from the grass to wonder
  Why by night and day the whim is still,
Why the silence is, and the stampers' thunder
  Sounds forth no more from the shattered mill.

In that whim he worked when the night winds
    bellowed
  On the riven summit of Giant's Hand,
And by day when prodigal Spring had yellowed
  All the wide, long sweep of enchanted land;
And he knew his shift, and the whistle's warning,
  And he knew the calls of the boys below;
Through the years, unbidden, at night or morning,
  He had taken his stand by the old whim bow.

But the whim stands still, and the wheeling swallow
  In the silent shaft hangs her home of clay,
And the lizards flirt and the swift snakes follow

O'er the grass-grown brace in the summer day;
And the corn springs high in the cracks and corners
   Of the forge, and down where the timber lies;
And the crows are perched like a band of mourners
   On the broken hut on the Hermit's Rise.

All the hands have gone, for the rich reef paid out,
   And the company waits till the calls come in;
But the old grey horse, like the claim, is played out,
   And no market's near for his bones and skin.
So they let him live, and they left him grazing
   By the creek, and oft in the evening dim
I have seen him stand on the rises, gazing
   At the ruined brace and the rotting whim.

The floods rush high in the gully under,
   And the lightnings lash at the shrinking trees,
Or the cattle down from the ranges blunder
   As the fires drive by on the summer breeze.
Still the feeble horse at the right hour wanders
   To the lonely ring, though the whistle's dumb,
And with hanging head by the bow he ponders
   Where the whim boy's gone — why the shifts
      don't come.

But there comes a night when he sees lights
      glowing
   In the roofless huts and the ravaged mill,
When he hears again all the stampers going —

Though the huts are dark and the stampers still:
When he sees the steam to the black roof clinging
  As its shadows roll on the silver sands,
And he knows the voice of his driver singing,
  And the knocker's clang where the braceman
    stands.

See the old horse take, like a creature dreaming,
  On the ring once more his accustomed place;
But the moonbeams full on the ruins streaming
  Show the scattered timbers and grass-grown
    brace.
Yet HE hears the sled in the smithy falling,
  And the empty truck as it rattles back,
And the boy who stands by the anvil, calling;
  And he turns and backs, and he 'takes up slack'.

While the old drum creaks, and the shadows shiver
  As the wind sweeps by, and the hut doors close,
And the bats dip down in the shaft or quiver
  In the ghostly light, round the grey horse goes;
And he feels the strain on his untouched shoulder,
  Hears again the voice that was dear to him,
Sees the form he knew — and his heart grows
    bolder
  As he works his shift by the broken whim.

He hears in the sluices the water rushing
  As the buckets drain and the doors fall back;

When the early dawn in the east is blushing,
  He is limping still round the old, old track.
Now he pricks his ears, with a neigh replying
  To a call unspoken, with eyes aglow,
And he sways and sinks in the circle, dying;
  From the ring no more will the grey horse go.

In a gully green, where a dam lies gleaming,
  And the bush creeps back on a worked-out claim,
And the sleepy crows in the sun sit dreaming
  On the timbers grey and a charred hut frame,
Where the legs slant down, and the hare is
    squatting
  In the high rank grass by the dried-up course,
Nigh a shattered drum and a king-post rotting
  Are the bleaching bones of the old grey horse.

GEOFFREY CHAUCER

from 'The Reeve's Tale'

This millere smyled of hir nycetee,
    And thoghte, 'Al this nys doon but for a wyle.
    They wene that no man may hem bigyle,
  But by my thrift, yet shal I blere hir ye,
    For al the sleighte in hir philosophye.
The moore queynte crekes that they make,
           The moore wol I stele whan I take.
In stide of flour yet wol I yeve hem bren.
  'The gretteste clerkes been noght wisest men,'
  As whilom to the wolf thus spak the mare.
  Of al hir art counte I noght a tare.'

  Out at the dore he gooth ful pryvely,
Whan that he saugh his tyme, softely.
  He looketh up and doun til he hath founde
    The clerkes hors, ther as it stood ybounde
    Bihynde the mille, under a levesel;
        And to the hors he goth hym faire and wel;
    He strepeth of the brydel right anon.
    And whan the hors was laus, he gynneth gon

Toward the fen, ther wilde mares renne,
  And forth with 'wehee,' thurgh thikke and
    thurgh thenne.

This millere gooth agayn, no word he seyde,
But dooth his note, and with the clerkes pleyde
Til that hir corn was faire and weel ygrounde.
And whan the mele is sakked and ybounde,
This John goth out and fynt his hors away,
And gan to crie 'Harrow!' and 'Weylaway!
Oure hors is lorn, Alayn, for Goddes banes,
Step on thy feet! Com of, man, al atanes!
Allas, our wardeyn has his palfrey lorn.'
This Aleyn al forgat, bothe mele and corn;

Al was out of his mynde his housbondrie.
'What, whilk way is he geen?' he gan to crie.
The wyf cam lepynge inward with a ren.
She seyde, 'Allas! youre hors goth to the fen
With wilde mares, as faste as he may go.
Unthank come on his hand that boond hym so,
And he that bettre sholde han knyt the reyne!'

'Allas,' quod John, 'Aleyn, for Cristes peyne
Lay doun thy swerd, and I wil myn alswa.

I is ful wight, God waat, as is a raa;
By Goddes herte, he sal nat scape us bathe!
Why ne had thow pit the capul in the lathe?
Ilhayl! By God, Alayn, thou is a fonne!'

Thise sely clerkes han ful faste yronne
Toward the fen, bothe Aleyn and eek John.

And whan the millere saugh that they were gon,
  He half a busshel of hir flour hath take,
          And bad his wyf go knede it in a cake.
  He seyde, 'I trowe the clerkes were aferd.

Yet kan a millere make a clerkes berd,

  For al his art; now lat hem goon hir weye!
      Lo, wher he gooth! Ye, lat the children pleye.
      They gete hym nat so lightly, by my croun.'

  Thise sely clerkes rennen up and doun
With 'Keep! Keep! Stand! Stand! Jossa, warderere,
      Ga whistle thou, and I shal kepe hym heere!'
         But shortly, til that it was verray nyght,
They koude nat, though they dide al hir myght,
  Hir capul cacche, he ran alwey so faste,
  Til in a dych they caughte hym atte laste.

  Wery and weet, as beest is in the reyn,
Comth sely John, and with him comth Aleyn.
      'Allas,' quod John, 'the day that I was born!
    Now are we dryve til hethyng and til scorn.
Oure corn is stoln; men wil us fooles calle,
      Bathe the wardeyn and oure felawes alle,
And namely the millere, weylaway!'
Thus pleyneth John as he gooth by the way
Toward the mille, and Bayard in his hond.
The millere sittynge by the fyr he fond,

For it was nyght, and forther myghte they noght;
But for the love of God they hym bisoght
Of herberwe and of ese, as for hir peny.

ROBERT WRIGLEY

Kissing a Horse

Of the two spoiled, barn-sour geldings
we owned that year, it was Red—
skittish and prone to explode
even at fourteen years—who'd let me
hold to my face his own: the massive labyrinthine
caverns of the nostrils, the broad plain
up the head to the eyes. He'd let me stroke
his coarse chin whiskers and take
his soft meaty underlip
in my hands, press my man's carnivorous
kiss to his grass-nipping upper half of one, just
so that I could smell
the long way his breath had come from the rain
and the sun, the lungs and the heart,
from a world that meant no harm.

Portrait of the Horse

Sometimes the horse is simply a horse.
 Sometimes the horse is a stalwart
 bearer of bodies.
 Sometimes the horse is stubborn,
 refusing to ford the river,
or the horse is a mistake
 in the vapor, what looks like a horse
 emerging out of a thrust
 of fog on Telegraph Avenue.
There's the perpetual feeling of being
 overdressed for summer
 and underdressed for spring.
 I'm variously sweat or shudder.
I mistake the strange bodies
for those I owe apologies to,
 oversleep and open my eyes on
 the clock radio, the time a typo,
 the apartment a disaster.
Sometimes the horse is a disaster
or the horse is time in a trot or a canter.
 Sometimes the horse is a boy
 growing in time into a man
 who often laments,

A horse, a horse, my kingdom, etc.
But there is no horse.
There are two days good and one day bad
without any hint of a horse.
Sometimes speaking about the horse
is a means of avoiding speaking
about myself which is lousy.
Late last night myself
regarding another carelessly.
Late last night my body
with a temporary body.
The horse is the taut metaphor for sex,
but sometimes the horse is the
taut silence after.
Sometimes the horse is the silence
after her body rises
in the embarrassment of morning
and leaves,
and this silence is filled
with less than remorse
but with more than indifference.
This is a feeling there is no word for.
What I decided in place of what I
needed.
I should eat better.
I should vacuum more often.
I should settle down
and raise a young horse.
Sometimes the horse is unspoken,

the horse is this feeling
that will be forgotten,

               is the self unable to alter its
                   ineffable horse.

Late last night, a pervasive clopping
of the horse on the hill.

               Late last night, the horse as a foghorn
               over the Bay.

                   I should be rained on.

                   I should not be forgiven.

The Horse's Adventure

The horse discovered a gateway to another
dimension, and with nothing else to do, moseyed
into it just for grins, and man, you
don't even want to know what happened
next—it was just, like, Horse at the French
Revolution. Horse in Franco's living room.
Horse on the moon. Horse in a supporting role
in an episode of ER. Horse being shot
out of a cannon. Horse on The Price Is Right.
Horse in a Whitesnake video. Horse
at Kennedy's assassination. Horse in the Tet
Offensive. Horse at the Gap gawking at some
khaki pants. Horse in Julie Piepmeyer's
bathroom. Horse being tossed out of an airplane
with a parachute strapped to its back, plummeting
toward Nebraska. Horse on Capitol Hill
(Yes, I'd like the floor to recognize
the distinguished horse from Arizona). Horse
on the subway. Horse authorizing a peace treaty
between the U.S. and Iraq. Horse
in the Evansville State Hospital. Horse caught up
in a White Hen robbery. Horse in the Kentucky
Derby. Horse staring at the merry-go-round

at King's Island in Cincinnati, Ohio.
The list goes on and on. And so goes
the horse's adventure, where one minute
it's standing next to Pat Sajak and with a violent
flash like that of a murderous camera or the twirling
screen and music of a Batman episode
it's standing in the middle of US-23
with a screaming motorist speeding toward it.
And this horse, whirling through dimension
after dimension, spiraling carmines, suicidal
jasmines, and mathematical theorems tornadoing
past it, being placed in situation
after situation—what had it learned
when all was said and done and it was back
at Tom Wallace's farm? Nothing is better
than Rachel Wallace while they stand in the barn
in the middle of February and she draws pictures of it
to take to school tomorrow.

Paternoster

Paternoster. Paternoster.
Hallowed be dy mane.
Dy kingdom come.
Dy draftwork be done.
Still plough the day
And give out daily bray
Though heart stiffen in the harness.
Then sleep hang harness with bearbells
And trot on bravely into sleep
Where the black and the bay
The sorrel and the grey
And foals and bearded wheat
Are waiting.
It is on earth as it is in heaven.
Drought, wildfire,
Wild asparagus, yellow flowers
On the flowering cactus.
Give our daily wheat, wet
Whiskers in the sonorous bucket.
Knead my heart, hardened daily.
Heal the hoofprint in my heart.
Give us our oats at bedtime
And in the night half-sleeping.

Paternoster. Paternoster.
Hallowed be dy hot mash.

JAMES WRIGHT

A Blessing

Just off the highway to Rochester, Minnesota,
Twilight bounds softly forth on the grass.
And the eyes of those two Indian ponies
Darken with kindness.
They have come gladly out of the willows
To welcome my friend and me.
We step over the barbed wire into the pasture
Where they have been grazing all day, alone.
They ripple tensely, they can hardly contain their
    happiness
That we have come.
They bow shyly as wet swans. They love each other.
There is no loneliness like theirs.
At home once more,
They begin munching the young tufts of spring in
    the darkness.
I would like to hold the slenderer one in my arms,
For she has walked over to me
And nuzzled my left hand.
She is black and white,
Her mane falls wild on her forehead,
And the light breeze moves me to caress her long
    ear

That is delicate as the skin over a girl's wrist.
Suddenly I realize
That if I stepped out of my body I would break
Into blossom.

Inventing a Horse

Inventing a horse is not easy.
One must not only think of the horse.
One must dig fence posts around him.
One must include a place where horses like to live;

or do when they live with humans like you.
Slowly, you must walk him in the cold;
feed him bran mash, apples;
accustom him to the harness;

holding in mind even when you are tired
harnesses and tack cloths and saddle oil
to keep the saddle clean as a face in the sun;
one must imagine teaching him to run

among the knuckles of tree roots,
not to be skittish at first sight of timber wolves,
and not to grow thin in the city,
where at some point you will have to live;

and one must imagine the absence of money.
Most of all, though: the living weight,
the sound of his feet on the needles,

and, since he is heavy, and real,

and sometimes tired after a run
down the river with a light whip at his side,
one must imagine love
in the mind that does not know love,

an animal mind, a love that does not depend
on your image of it,
your understanding of it;
indifferent to all that it lacks:

a muzzle and two black eyes
looking the day away, a field empty
of everything but witchgrass, fluent trees,
and some piles of hay.

Horses in Snow

They are a gift I have wanted again.
Wanted: One moment in mountains
when winter got so cold
the oil froze before it could burn.
I chopped ferns of hoarfrost from all the windows
and peered up at pines, a wedding cake
by a baker gone mad. Swirls by the thousand
shimmered above me until a cloud
lumbered over a ridge,
bringing the heavier white of more flurries.

I believed, I believed, I believed
it would last, that when you went out
to test the black ice or to dig out a Volkswagon
filled with rich women, you'd return
and we'd sputter like oil,
match after match, warm in the making.
Wisconsin's flat farmland never approved:
I hid in cornfields far into October,
listening to music that whirled from my
   thumbprint.
When sunset played havoc with bright leaves of
   alders,

I never mentioned longing or fear.
I crouched like a good refugee in brown creeks
and forgot why Autumn is harder than Spring.
But snug on the western slope of that mountain
I'd accept every terror, break open seals
to release love's headwaters to unhurried sunlight.
Weren't we Big Hearts? Through some trick of silver
we held one another, believing each motion the real
     one,
ah, lover, why were dark sources bundled up
in our eyes? Each owned an agate,

marbled with anguish, a heart or its echo,
we hardly knew. Lips touching lips,
did that break my horizon
as much as those horses broke my belief?
You drove off and I walked the old road,
scolding the doubles that wanted so much.
The chestnut mare whinnied a cloud into scrub
     pine.
In a windless corner of a corral,
four horses fit like puzzle pieces.
Their dark eyes and lashes defined by the white.

The colt kicked his hind, loped from the fence.
The mares and a stallion galloped behind,
lifting and leaping, finding each other
in full accord with the earth and their bodies.
No harm ever touched them once they cut loose,

snorting at flurries falling again.
How little our chances for feeling ourselves.
They vanished so quickly—one flick of a tail.
Where do their mountains and moments begin?
I stood a long time in sharpening wind.

Winnie

When I went by the meadow gate
The chestnut mare would trot to meet me,
And as her coming I would wait,
She'd whinney high as if to greet me.
And I would kiss her silky nose,
And stroke her neck until it glistened,
And speak soft words: I don't suppose
She understand – but how she listened!

Then in the war-net I was caught,
Returning three black winters older;
And when the little mare I sought
The farmer told me he had sold her.
And so time passed – when in the street
One day I heard a plaintive whinney
That roused a recollection sweet,
So then I turned and there was Winnie.

I vow she knew me, mooning there.
She raised her nose for me to fondle,
And though I'd lost an arm I'll swear
She kissed the empty sleeve a-dangle.
But oh it cut me to the heart,

Though I was awful glad to meet her,
For lo! she dragged a tinker's cart
And stumbled weakly as he beat her.

Just skin and bone, a sorry hack!
Say, fellow, you may think it funny:

I made a deal and bought her back,

Though it took all my bonus money.
And she'll be in the meadow there,
As long as I have dough for spending ...
Gee! I'll take care of that old mare –
'Sweetheart! you'll have a happy ending.'

VICKI HEARNE

Riding a Nervous Horse

A dozen false starts:
You're such a fool, I said,
Spooking at shadows when
All day you were calm,
Placidly nosing the bushes
That now you pretend are strange,
Are struck with menace.

But he shuddered, stubborn
In his horsy posture,
Saying that I brought
Devils with me that he
Could hear gathering in all
The places behind him as I
Diverted his coherence
With my chatter and tack.

Indeed I have stolen
Something, a careful attention
I claim for my own yearning
Purpose, while he
Is left alone to guard
Us both from horse eaters

That merely grin at me
But I lust for him, for
The beauty of the haunch
My brush has polished, revealing
Treasures of edible light
In the shift of hide and hooves.

Sources

EAVAN BOLAND, 'The War Horse' from *New Collected Poems*. 'The War Horse' was first published in 1975 by Gollancz London, now an imprint of Orion Publishing Group. Reprinted with permission from Carcanet Press.

JASWINDER BOLINA, 'Portrait of the Horse' from *Phantom Camera*. Copyright © 2013 by Jaswinder Bolina, reprinted with permission from New Issues Poetry & Prose.

JASON BREDLE, 'The Horse's Adventure' from *Standing in Line for the Beast*. Copyright © 2007 by Jason Bredle, reprinted with permission from New Issues Poetry & Prose.

JENNIFER CHANG, 'A Horse Named Never', from *Some Say the Lark: Poems*. Copyright © 2017 by

of Vicki Hearne's Literary Estate (Robert
Tragesser).

JANE HIRSHFIELD, 'Heat' from *Of Gravity and Angels*.
Copyright © 1998 by Jane Hirschfield. Published
by Wesleyan University Press and reprinted with
permission.

TED HUGHES, 'The Horses' from *Collected Poems of Ted
Hughes*, ed. Paul Keegan. Copyright © The Estate
of Ted Hughes, 2003, reprinted with permission
of Faber & Faber Ltd.

Extract from 'Sir Gawain and the Green Knight'
from *Sir Gawain and the Green Knight*, The
Pearl Poet (Author), A. S. Kline (Translator).
Copyright © 2007.

PHILIP LARKIN, 'At Grass' from *The Less Deceived* (The
Marvell Press, 1955). Reprinted with permission
from Faber & Faber Ltd.

EDWIN MUIR, 'The Horses' from *Selected Poems*.
Reprinted with permission from Faber & Faber
Ltd.

PAUL MULDOON, 'Bull Run' from 'Horse Latitudes',
Horse Latitudes. Reprinted with permission from
Faber & Faber Ltd.

WILLIAM HENRY OGILVIE, 'The Horse of Your Heart',
featured in *A Handful of Leather* and *The Collected
Sporting Verse*, reprinted with permission from
Will H. Ogilvie Archive and Catherine Reid.

MARY OLIVER, 'Franz Marc's Blue Horses', from